Table Of Contents

I. Introduction

A. The demand for versatile software engineers

B. Overview of the book's purpose and goals

II. Understanding the Role of Backend and Frontend Software Engineers

A. Explaining the differences between backend and frontend development

B. Highlighting the importance of being proficient in both areas

C. Advantages of being a full-stack software engineer

III. Building a Strong Foundation

A. Basic programming concepts and languages

B. Essential web development technologies

C. Data structures and algorithms for backend and frontend

IV. Backend Development

A. Exploring backend technologies and frameworks

B. Database management and design principles

C. Server-side scripting and API development

D. Security considerations in backend development

V. Frontend Development

A. Introduction to frontend technologies and frameworks

B. User interface (UI) design principles and best practices

C. Building responsive and accessible web interfaces

D. Integrating backend functionality with frontend

VI. Bridging the Gap: Full-Stack Development

A. Understanding the interplay between backend and frontend

B. Creating seamless integration between the two layers

C. Managing data flow and communication between server and client

VII. Tools, Frameworks, and Libraries

A. Overview of popular tools and frameworks for backend and frontend

B. How to choose the right technology stack for your projects

C. Best practices for working with common libraries and APIs

VIII. Project-Based Learning

A. Designing and implementing a full-stack project

B. Step-by-step walkthrough of a practical application

C. Applying best practices and industry standards

IX. Continuous Learning and Professional Growth

A. Staying updated with the latest technologies and trends

B. Participating in open-source projects and communities

C. Leveraging online resources for ongoing learning

X. Career Paths and Opportunities

A. Exploring various career paths for full-stack engineers

B. Job market trends and demand for versatile developers

C. Advancement opportunities and potential future roles

XI. Conclusion

A. Recap of key concepts covered in the book

B. Encouragement and guidance for aspiring full-stack engineers

C. Final thoughts and next steps for readers

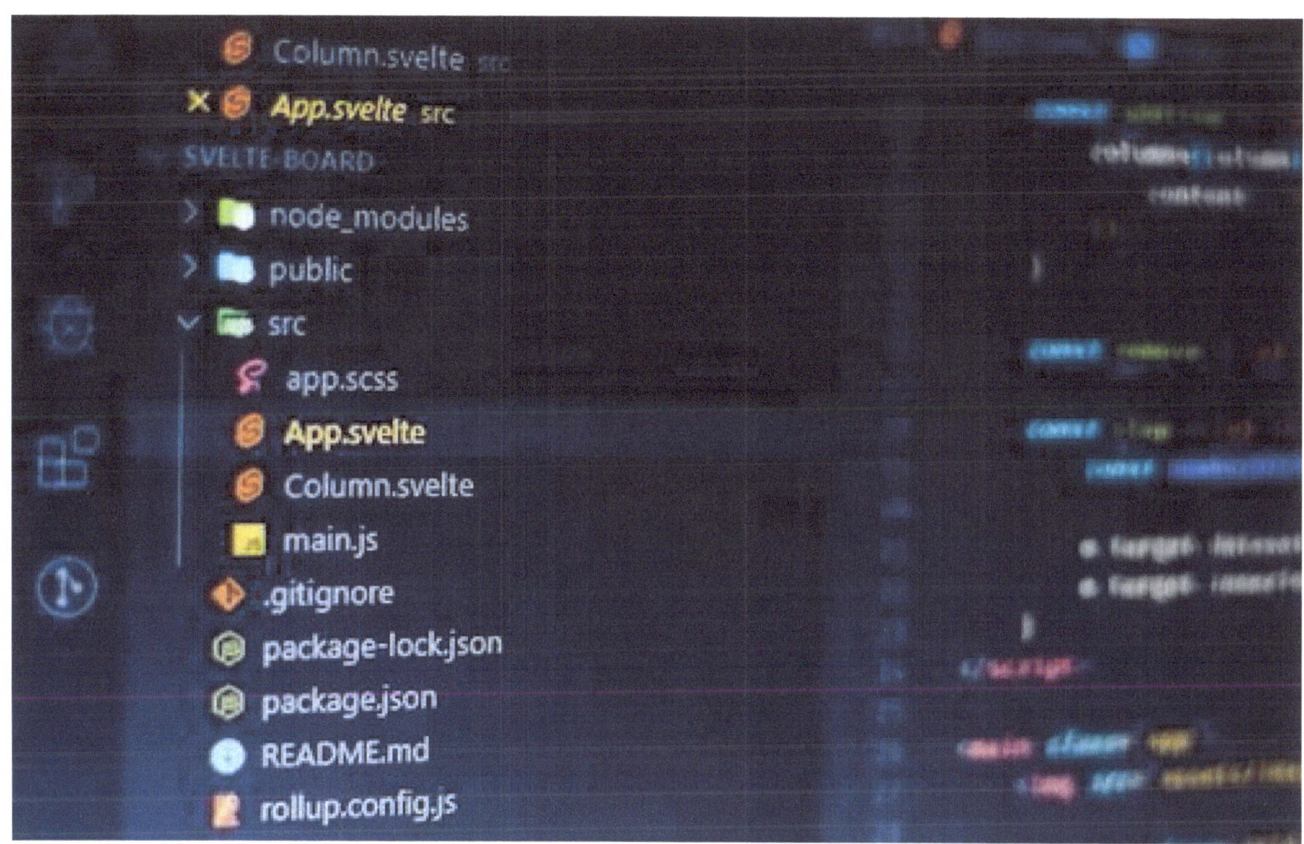

Chapter I. Introduction

A. The demand for versatile software engineers

In today's rapidly evolving digital landscape, the demand for skilled software engineers is higher than ever before. With businesses relying heavily on technology to streamline their operations and connect with customers, there is a pressing need for professionals who possess a comprehensive understanding of both backend and frontend development. This need has given rise to the emergence of full-stack software engineers, individuals who are proficient in both the server-side and client-side aspects of software development.

Traditionally, software engineers have been categorized into either backend or frontend specialists, each focusing on a specific aspect of the application development process. Backend developers work behind the scenes, building the server-side logic, managing databases, and ensuring data integrity and security. On the other hand, frontend developers are responsible for crafting user interfaces that are visually appealing, intuitive, and responsive to user interactions.

While specialization has its merits, the demand for versatile professionals who can bridge the gap between backend and frontend development has increased significantly. Employers are seeking individuals who can handle the entire software development lifecycle, from designing robust architectures to creating seamless user experiences. By mastering both backend and frontend skills, software engineers can position themselves as invaluable assets in the ever-evolving tech industry.

B. Overview of the book's purpose and goals

The purpose of this book, "How to Become Both a Backend and Frontend Software Engineer," is to guide aspiring developers on the path to becoming proficient in both backend and frontend development. It aims to equip readers with the knowledge, skills, and mindset necessary to navigate the challenges and complexities of working in the full-stack software engineering domain.

This book is designed to be a comprehensive resource that covers the fundamental concepts, tools, and best practices of backend and frontend development. Whether you are a beginner starting your journey in software engineering or an experienced developer looking to expand your skill set, this book will provide you with the guidance and practical insights needed to become a proficient full-stack software engineer.

Throughout the chapters, we will explore the different aspects of backend and frontend development, from understanding the underlying technologies and frameworks to building robust applications that seamlessly integrate server-side and client-side functionality. By following the step-by-step tutorials and engaging in project-based learning, readers will gain hands-on experience in working with various technologies, allowing them to apply their newfound knowledge in real-world scenarios.

Additionally, this book will delve into career paths and opportunities available for full-stack software engineers, providing insights into the job market, industry trends, and potential future roles. It will also emphasize the importance of continuous learning and professional growth, encouraging readers to stay updated with the latest technologies and participate in open-source projects and communities.

By the end of this book, readers will have a solid foundation in both backend and frontend development, enabling them to pursue fulfilling careers as full-stack software engineers. They will possess the necessary skills to design, build, and maintain robust software applications, seamlessly integrating backend and frontend components to deliver exceptional user experiences.

Whether you aspire to work in small startups, large corporations, or as a freelance developer, this book will equip you with the knowledge and tools needed to succeed in today's competitive tech industry. So, let's embark on this journey together and unlock the vast opportunities that await those who master the art of being both a backend and frontend software engineer.

Chapter II. Understanding the Role of Backend and Frontend Software Engineers

A. Explaining the Differences between Backend and Frontend Development

To lay a solid foundation for becoming a proficient full-stack software engineer, it is essential to understand the distinctions between backend and frontend development. Backend development primarily focuses on the server-side aspects of software applications. Backend engineers are responsible for handling data storage, managing databases, implementing business logic, and ensuring the overall functionality and performance of the application. They work with programming languages like Python, Java, Ruby, or frameworks such as Node.js and Django to build the server-side components.

In contrast, frontend development centers around the client-side aspects of an application—the part that users directly interact with. Frontend engineers are responsible for designing and implementing user interfaces (UI) and user experiences (UX). They work with technologies like HTML, CSS, and JavaScript to create visually appealing and interactive interfaces that provide seamless user interactions. Additionally, they may utilize frontend frameworks such as React, Angular, or Vue.js to enhance the development process and create responsive web applications.

B. Highlighting the Importance of Being Proficient in Both Areas

While specializing in either backend or frontend development can be valuable, there are several compelling reasons to become proficient in both areas:

1.Versatility and Adaptability: As a full-stack software engineer, you possess a broader skill set, allowing you to handle a wide range of development tasks. This versatility enables you to adapt to different project requirements, switch between roles, and contribute effectively to various stages of the software development lifecycle.

2.Efficient Collaboration: Understanding both backend and frontend development allows you to communicate effectively with specialists in each area. You can bridge the communication gap between backend and frontend teams, facilitate collaboration, and contribute to more streamlined and efficient development processes.

3.End-to-End Application Development: Being proficient in both areas empowers you to take charge of the entire development process, from designing the architecture to implementing the user interface. This holistic perspective enables you to create cohesive and integrated applications, ensuring a seamless user experience and efficient data flow between the server and the client.

4.Problem Solving and Troubleshooting: When issues arise during development, having knowledge of both backend and frontend allows you to identify and address problems more effectively. You can understand the entire system's workings, trace the root cause of an issue, and implement appropriate solutions, saving time and effort in the troubleshooting process.

C. Advantages of Being a Full-Stack Software Engineer

Becoming a full-stack software engineer brings numerous advantages that can benefit your career and professional growth:

1.Expanded Career Opportunities: Full-stack software engineers are in high demand due to their ability to handle diverse tasks and contribute to various aspects of the development process. This broad skill set opens up a wide range of career opportunities, whether you choose to work in startups, established companies, or pursue freelance projects.

2.Increased Autonomy and Flexibility: With proficiency in both backend and frontend development, you gain greater autonomy and flexibility in your work. You can take ownership of projects, make informed decisions, and effectively manage the entire development lifecycle independently or as part of a team.

3.Professional Growth and Learning: By embracing the challenges of full-stack development, you embark on a continuous learning journey. You stay updated with the latest technologies, frameworks, and best practices in both backend and frontend domains, enhancing your professional growth and ensuring long-term career relevance.

4.Enhanced Problem-Solving Skills: Full-stack software engineers develop strong problem-solving skills by tackling challenges across the entire application stack. You learn to think critically, analyze complex problems, and find innovative solutions, making you a valuable asset in any development team.

5.Adaptability to Technological Shifts: The tech industry constantly evolves, and new technologies and frameworks emerge regularly. Full-stack software engineers are better equipped to adapt to these shifts as they can quickly learn and apply new technologies in both backend and frontend development, ensuring their skills remain up-to-date and marketable.

In summary, understanding the distinctions between backend and frontend development and recognizing the importance of being proficient in both areas lays the groundwork for becoming a full-stack software engineer. Embracing this role brings numerous advantages, including versatility, efficient collaboration, end-to-end application development capabilities, effective problem-solving skills, expanded career opportunities, autonomy, and continuous professional growth. With this knowledge, you are ready to delve deeper into the essential concepts, technologies, and best practices of backend and frontend development, setting the stage for your journey towards becoming a proficient full-stack software engineer.

Chapter III. Building a Strong Foundation

A. Basic Programming Concepts and Languages

Building a strong foundation in software engineering begins with understanding basic programming concepts and familiarizing yourself with essential programming languages. These concepts serve as the building blocks for backend and frontend development and provide a solid framework for mastering more advanced topics. Here are some key areas to focus on:

1.Variables and Data Types: Learn how to declare variables and understand different data types such as numbers, strings, booleans, and arrays. Familiarize yourself with variable scope, data type conversions, and type checking.

Control Flow: Gain proficiency in control flow statements such as conditionals (if-else, switch), loops (for, while), and exception handling. Understand how to use these statements to control the flow of program execution.

2.Functions and Methods: Explore the concept of functions and methods, including parameter passing, return values, and function overloading. Learn how to write reusable code by encapsulating logic within functions.

3.Object-Oriented Programming (OOP): Master the principles of OOP, including classes, objects, inheritance, polymorphism, and encapsulation. Understand how to design and implement robust software using OOP concepts.

4.Error Handling and Debugging: Develop skills in identifying and handling errors, and use debugging techniques and tools to troubleshoot code issues effectively.

5.Version Control: Learn how to use version control systems like Git to track changes, collaborate with others, and manage code repositories.

As for programming languages, focus on foundational languages commonly used in backend and frontend development, such as:

Backend: Python, Java, Ruby, C#, PHP

Frontend: JavaScript, HTML, CSS

B. Essential Web Development Technologies

To become a proficient full-stack software engineer, it is crucial to gain a solid understanding of essential web development technologies. These technologies form the backbone of web applications and empower developers to create interactive and dynamic web experiences. Here are key areas to explore:

HTML: Learn the structure and semantics of HTML (Hypertext Markup Language), which is the foundation for creating web pages. Understand how to use tags, attributes, and elements to structure content and define the visual presentation of web pages.

CSS: Familiarize yourself with CSS (Cascading Style Sheets), a language used to describe the look and formatting of

HTML documents. Learn how to apply styles, define layouts, and create responsive designs to enhance the visual presentation of web pages.

JavaScript: Master JavaScript, a versatile programming language for creating interactive and dynamic web content. Understand the basics of JavaScript, including variables, functions, loops, and conditionals. Learn how to manipulate the Document Object Model (DOM) to handle user interactions and dynamically update web page content.

HTTP and REST: Gain knowledge of the HTTP (Hypertext Transfer Protocol) protocol and its role in client-server communication. Understand the principles of REST (Representational State Transfer) and how it facilitates the design of web APIs.

Web Servers: Explore web servers such as Apache and Nginx, and learn how they handle incoming requests and serve web content. Understand concepts like routing, handling HTTP methods (GET, POST, etc.), and server-side configurations.

Browser Developer Tools: Familiarize yourself with browser developer tools, such as the Chrome DevTools, which provide debugging capabilities, performance analysis, and inspection of web pages and applications.

C. Data Structures and Algorithms for Backend and Frontend

A strong foundation in data structures and algorithms is essential for both backend and frontend development. These concepts enable you to write efficient code, optimize performance, and solve complex problems. Here are key areas to focus on:

1.Data Structures: Learn about fundamental data structures such as arrays, linked lists, stacks, queues, trees, graphs, and hash tables. Understand their properties, operations, and time complexity analysis.

2.Algorithms: Study common algorithms like searching, sorting, traversal, recursion, and dynamic programming. Explore algorithm design paradigms, such as divide and conquer, greedy algorithms, and backtracking.

3.Database Basics: Understand the basics of relational databases, including concepts like tables, entities, attributes, and relationships. Explore Structured Query Language (SQL) for data manipulation and retrieval.

4.Performance Analysis: Learn how to analyze algorithm efficiency using Big O notation. Understand concepts like time complexity, space complexity, and how to optimize code for better performance.

5.Caching: Gain knowledge of caching mechanisms and strategies to improve application performance. Understand how to leverage caching techniques effectively, such as in-memory caching and content delivery networks (CDNs).

By building a strong foundation in basic programming concepts and languages, essential web development technologies, and data structures and algorithms, you will have the groundwork necessary to excel in both backend and frontend development. These core concepts will serve as your toolkit as you dive deeper into the world of full-stack software engineering, enabling you to design robust applications, optimize performance, and solve complex problems effectively.

Chapter IV. Backend Development

A. Exploring Backend Technologies and Frameworks

Backend development forms the backbone of any software application, handling server-side logic, data management, and ensuring smooth functionality. To become a proficient full-stack software engineer, it is crucial to explore various backend technologies and frameworks. Here are some key areas to delve into:

1.Server-Side Languages: Familiarize yourself with popular server-side programming languages such as Python, Java, Ruby, C#, and PHP. Understand their syntax, features, and ecosystem. Explore their strengths and weaknesses in different use cases.

2.Backend Frameworks: Explore backend frameworks that simplify and accelerate the development process. Examples include Django (Python), Spring Boot (Java), Ruby on Rails (Ruby), ASP.NET (C#), and Laravel (PHP). Learn how to leverage these frameworks to build robust and scalable backend applications.

3.Application Servers: Gain knowledge of application servers like Apache Tomcat, Nginx, and Microsoft Internet Information Services (IIS). Understand their role in serving web applications and handling requests from clients.

4.Containerization: Explore containerization technologies such as Docker, which allow for the efficient deployment and scaling of backend applications. Learn how to package applications and their dependencies into containers, ensuring consistent deployment across different environments.

5.Cloud Services: Familiarize yourself with cloud platforms like Amazon Web Services (AWS), Microsoft Azure, and Google Cloud Platform (GCP). Understand how to leverage cloud services for hosting, scaling, and managing backend applications in a distributed environment.

B. Database Management and Design Principles

Database management is a critical aspect of backend development, responsible for storing, retrieving, and managing data. Understanding database design principles and techniques is essential for building robust and scalable applications. Here are key areas to focus on:

1.Relational Databases: Learn about relational database management systems (RDBMS) like MySQL, PostgreSQL, and Oracle. Understand concepts such as tables, primary keys, foreign keys, normalization, and query optimization.

2.NoSQL Databases: Explore non-relational databases like MongoDB, Cassandra, and Redis. Understand their characteristics, data modeling approaches, and use cases where NoSQL databases excel.

3.Database Design: Learn how to design efficient database schemas, taking into account data integrity, performance, and scalability. Understand concepts like entity-relationship (ER) modeling and database normalization.

4.Query Languages: Master SQL (Structured Query Language) for data manipulation and retrieval. Learn how to write efficient queries, utilize indexes, and optimize database performance.

5.ORM (Object-Relational Mapping): Familiarize yourself with ORM frameworks like Hibernate (Java), SQLAlchemy (Python), and Entity Framework (C#). Understand how ORM simplifies database interaction by mapping database records to objects.

C. Server-Side Scripting and API Development

Server-side scripting and API development are integral parts of backend development, enabling communication between the server and client applications. Here are key areas to explore:

Server-Side Scripting: Understand server-side scripting languages such as PHP, Ruby, or Node.js. Learn how to write server-side scripts to handle requests, process data, and generate dynamic web content.

1.RESTful APIs: Gain knowledge of building RESTful APIs (Representational State Transfer) that follow a standardized architectural style. Learn how to design resource-oriented endpoints, handle

HTTP methods (GET, POST, PUT, DELETE), and handle authentication and authorization.

2.API Frameworks: Explore popular API frameworks like Express.js (Node.js), Flask (Python), and Ruby on Rails (Ruby). Understand how these frameworks simplify API development, routing, input validation, and response handling.

3.Authentication and Authorization: Learn about authentication mechanisms such as token-based authentication (JWT) and OAuth. Understand how to secure APIs, handle user sessions, and implement role-based access control.

4.API Documentation: Familiarize yourself with tools like Swagger and OpenAPI specifications to generate comprehensive and interactive API documentation. Learn the importance of documenting APIs for seamless integration with client applications.

D. Security Considerations in Backend Development

Security is a critical aspect of backend development, ensuring the protection of sensitive data, preventing unauthorized access, and defending against malicious attacks. Here are key areas to focus on:

1.Secure Coding Practices: Understand secure coding principles, such as input validation, output encoding, and protection against common vulnerabilities like SQL injection, cross-site scripting (XSS), and cross-site request forgery (CSRF).

2.User Authentication and Authorization: Learn about secure authentication mechanisms, including hashing and salting passwords, implementing multi-factor authentication, and session management. Understand authorization techniques to control access to sensitive resources.

3.Data Encryption: Explore techniques for encrypting sensitive data at rest and in transit. Understand how to use cryptographic algorithms and libraries to protect data integrity and confidentiality.

4.Security Auditing and Testing: Learn about security auditing and penetration testing methodologies to identify vulnerabilities in backend applications. Understand how to perform security assessments and implement best practices to secure your application.

5.Compliance and Regulations: Familiarize yourself with industry-specific compliance standards and regulations, such as Payment Card Industry Data Security Standard (PCI DSS) or General Data Protection Regulation (GDPR). Understand how to adhere to these standards in backend development.

By exploring backend technologies and frameworks, mastering database management and design principles, delving into server-side scripting and API development, and understanding security considerations, you will gain the necessary skills to build robust, secure, and scalable backend applications. These competencies are essential for becoming a proficient full-stack software engineer and creating seamless integration between backend and frontend components of an application.

Chapter V. Frontend Development

A. Introduction to Frontend Technologies and Frameworks

Frontend development focuses on creating visually appealing and interactive user interfaces (UI) that provide seamless user experiences. To become a proficient full-stack software engineer, it is essential to explore various frontend technologies and frameworks. Here are key areas to delve into:

HTML: Understand the structure and semantics of HTML (Hypertext Markup Language). Learn how to use tags, attributes, and elements to create the foundation of web pages.

CSS: Familiarize yourself with CSS (Cascading Style Sheets), which is used for styling and layout. Learn how to apply styles, manage typography, handle layouts, and create responsive designs.

JavaScript: Master JavaScript, a versatile programming language for frontend development. Understand its syntax, data types, functions, and object-oriented capabilities. Learn how to manipulate the Document Object Model (DOM) to dynamically update web content.

Frontend Frameworks: Explore popular frontend frameworks such as React, Angular, and Vue.js. Understand their core concepts, component-based architectures, and how they simplify UI development.

State Management: Learn about state management libraries like Redux (for React) or NgRx (for Angular). Understand how to manage application state and facilitate data flow between components.

B. User Interface (UI) Design Principles and Best Practices

Creating an intuitive and visually appealing user interface is crucial for frontend development. Understanding UI design principles and best practices will help you craft engaging and user-friendly experiences. Here are key areas to focus on:

Visual Hierarchy: Learn how to structure UI elements to guide users' attention and prioritize information effectively. Understand the use of typography, colors, and whitespace to create a clear visual hierarchy.

Responsive Design: Master the art of building responsive interfaces that adapt to different screen sizes and devices. Learn about media queries, fluid layouts, and techniques like mobile-first design.

User Experience (UX) Design: Explore UX design principles, including user research, wireframing, prototyping, and usability testing. Understand the importance of user-centered design and how to create engaging experiences.

Accessibility: Familiarize yourself with accessibility guidelines (such as WCAG 2.1) and learn how to create web interfaces that are inclusive and accessible to users with disabilities. Understand techniques for enhancing keyboard navigation, providing alternative text for images, and ensuring proper semantic markup.

Performance Optimization: Learn techniques to optimize frontend performance, such as minimizing file sizes, reducing HTTP requests, and leveraging caching mechanisms. Understand the importance of code optimization, lazy loading, and image optimization.

C. Building Responsive and Accessible Web Interfaces

Creating responsive and accessible web interfaces is vital to ensure an optimal user experience across different devices and user needs. Here are key areas to explore:

Responsive Web Design: Understand the principles of responsive web design, including fluid grids, flexible images, and media queries. Learn how to create layouts that adapt to different screen sizes and orientations.

CSS Frameworks: Explore CSS frameworks like Bootstrap, Foundation, or Tailwind CSS. Learn how to leverage pre-built components and responsive grids to speed up frontend development and maintain consistency.

Mobile Development: Gain knowledge of mobile-specific development considerations, such as touch events, mobile-specific UI components, and offline capabilities using Progressive Web Apps (PWA).

Cross-Browser Compatibility: Learn techniques for ensuring cross-browser compatibility, including feature detection, graceful degradation, and vendor prefixing. Understand how to test and optimize frontend code across different browsers.

Web Accessibility: Deepen your understanding of web accessibility principles and techniques. Learn how to implement accessible forms, provide proper document structure, and utilize

ARIA (Accessible Rich Internet Applications) attributes.

D. Integrating Backend Functionality with Frontend

In full-stack development, integrating backend functionality with the frontend is crucial to create seamless and functional applications. Here are key areas to focus on:

API Consumption: Learn how to consume APIs (Application Programming Interfaces) to fetch data from the backend. Understand techniques such as AJAX (Asynchronous JavaScript and XML), fetch API, and libraries like Axios.

Data Manipulation: Master techniques for manipulating and processing data received from the backend. Understand how to transform and format data to meet frontend requirements, utilizing JavaScript's array methods and libraries like Lodash.

Routing and Navigation: Explore frontend routing libraries like React Router or Angular Router. Learn how to handle navigation between different views, passing data through routes, and handling route guards.

State Synchronization: Understand techniques for synchronizing frontend state with backend data. Learn about concepts like two-way data binding, unidirectional data flow, and handling asynchronous updates using techniques like polling or WebSocket.

Error Handling and Feedback: Learn how to handle errors and provide feedback to users when interacting with backend functionality. Understand error response handling, validation messages, and displaying loading states.

By exploring frontend technologies and frameworks, understanding UI design principles and best practices, building responsive and accessible web interfaces, and integrating backend functionality with the frontend, you will gain the necessary skills to create immersive and seamless user experiences. This knowledge is essential for becoming a proficient full-stack software engineer, capable of developing robust applications that combine the power of backend functionality with intuitive frontend interfaces.

Chapter VI. Bridging the Gap: Full-Stack Development

A. Understanding the Interplay between Backend and Frontend

Full-stack development involves understanding and effectively bridging the gap between backend and frontend development. To become a proficient full-stack software engineer, it is essential to comprehend the interplay between these two layers of an application. Here are key areas to explore:

Data Flow: Understand how data flows between the server and the client. Learn about the Request-Response cycle, where the client sends a request to the server, and the server responds with the requested data. Comprehend the different HTTP methods (GET, POST, PUT, DELETE) and how they interact with backend APIs.

Frontend-Backend Communication: Explore techniques for frontend-backend communication, such as making API calls from the frontend to retrieve or send data. Understand how to handle responses and errors, parse data, and update the frontend interface accordingly.

Backend-Frontend Interaction: Gain insights into how the backend interacts with the frontend. Understand how to provide data from the server to the frontend, handle user input, and trigger backend operations based on user actions.

Synchronization and Real-Time Updates: Learn about techniques for synchronizing data between the frontend and backend in real-time. Understand concepts like

WebSockets and event-driven architectures to enable real-time updates and bidirectional communication.

B. Creating Seamless Integration between the Two Layers

Creating a seamless integration between the backend and frontend is crucial for building efficient and cohesive applications. Here are key areas to focus on:

API Design and Documentation: Understand how to design APIs that provide clear and consistent interfaces for frontend developers. Learn about API versioning, proper resource naming, and designing endpoints to optimize frontend-backend interaction. Also, emphasize the importance of documenting APIs for clear communication between backend and frontend teams.

Cross-Team Collaboration: Foster effective collaboration between backend and frontend teams. Encourage regular communication, knowledge sharing, and alignment on project goals. Explore agile methodologies that promote cross-functional teams and close collaboration between all stakeholders.

Code Organization and Modularization: Learn how to organize codebases in a modular and reusable manner. Understand the importance of separation of concerns and adhering to coding best practices. Emphasize the use of frontend build tools and bundlers to optimize the development process and minimize dependencies.

Component-based Architecture: Adopt component-based architectures like React components or Angular components. Understand how to break down the user interface into reusable and modular components. Explore techniques for passing data and events between components to maintain a cohesive and responsive application.

C. Managing Data Flow and Communication between Server and Client

Efficiently managing data flow and communication between the server and client is crucial for full-stack development. Here are key areas to explore:

State Management: Understand how to manage application state across the backend and frontend layers. Explore techniques such as server-side session management, frontend state management libraries (e.g., Redux, NgRx), and local storage.

Asynchronous Programming: Gain proficiency in asynchronous programming techniques to handle server-client interactions. Learn about promises, async/await syntax, and handling asynchronous operations effectively to prevent blocking and improve performance.

Validation and Error Handling: Implement validation mechanisms to ensure data integrity and prevent invalid data from being processed. Learn about client-side validation and backend validation techniques, including error handling and feedback to users.

Performance Optimization: Explore techniques for optimizing data transfer and improving application performance. Understand concepts like lazy loading, server-side caching, and minimizing network requests to reduce latency and improve user experience.

Testing and Debugging: Master testing and debugging techniques for both backend and frontend components. Understand how to write unit tests, integration tests, and end-to-end tests to ensure the seamless integration and functionality of the entire application stack.

By understanding the interplay between backend and frontend, creating seamless integration between the two layers, and effectively managing data flow and communication, you will become proficient in full-stack development. This knowledge enables you to design and build applications that provide a cohesive user experience, leveraging the strengths of both backend and frontend technologies. With these skills, you can confidently navigate the challenges of full-stack development and deliver robust and integrated software solutions.

Chapter VII. Tools, Frameworks, and Libraries

A. Overview of Popular Tools and Frameworks for Backend and Frontend

In the fast-paced world of software development, leveraging the right tools, frameworks, and libraries is crucial for efficient and effective development. In this chapter, we will explore popular tools and frameworks for both backend and frontend development. By understanding these technologies, you can enhance your productivity and build robust applications. Here are key areas to explore:

Backend Tools and Frameworks:

a. **Express.js:** A minimal and flexible Node.js framework for building fast and scalable web applications.

b. **Django:** A high-level Python web framework that follows the Model-View-Controller (MVC) architectural pattern.

c. Ruby on Rails: A popular Ruby framework that promotes convention over configuration and emphasizes developer productivity. d. Spring Boot: A Java framework that simplifies the development of stand-alone, production-grade Spring applications.

Frontend Tools and Frameworks:

a. React: A JavaScript library for building user interfaces with a component-based approach and a virtual DOM.

b. Angular: A TypeScript-based framework for building scalable and robust web applications with a focus on structured architecture.

c. Vue.js: A progressive JavaScript framework that is approachable, versatile, and easy to integrate into existing projects. d. Svelte: A lightweight framework that compiles components at build time, resulting in highly performant web applications.

Development Tools:

a. Visual Studio Code: A popular lightweight and extensible code editor with rich language support and a vast extension ecosystem.

b. Git: A distributed version control system that allows for efficient collaboration and code management.

c. Postman: A powerful API testing and development tool that simplifies API interactions and enables automated testing.

B. How to Choose the Right Technology Stack for Your Projects

Selecting the right technology stack is critical to the success of your projects. The technology stack encompasses the combination of programming languages, frameworks, libraries, and tools that you choose to build your application. Here are key factors to consider when choosing a technology stack:

1.Project Requirements: Understand the specific requirements of your project.

Consider factors such as scalability, performance, security, and compatibility with existing systems.

2.Learning Curve and Familiarity: Evaluate your familiarity with different technologies and frameworks. Consider the learning curve involved in adopting a new technology and the availability of resources for learning and support.

3.Community and Ecosystem: Assess the community support and ecosystem around a technology stack. Look for active communities, documentation, and a rich selection of libraries and resources that can accelerate development.

4.Team Skills and Expertise: Consider the skills and expertise of your development team. Evaluate their proficiency in different technologies and their ability to support and maintain the chosen stack.

5.Long-Term Viability: Look for technologies with a strong track record and active development. Consider factors such as community adoption, industry trends, and long-term support to ensure the stack remains relevant in the future.

C. Best Practices for Working with Common Libraries and APIs

Working with libraries and APIs is an integral part of modern software development. These resources help streamline development, enhance functionality, and provide ready-made solutions. Here are some best practices for working with common libraries and APIs:

1.Documentation: Read and understand the documentation of the library or API thoroughly. Documentation provides valuable insights into usage, features, and best practices.

2.Versioning: Pay attention to library or API versioning. Understand how to manage and update dependencies to ensure compatibility and leverage new features.

3.Error Handling: Implement robust error handling mechanisms when working with libraries or APIs. Handle exceptions gracefully and provide meaningful error messages for effective debugging.

4.Security Considerations: Understand the security implications of using libraries or APIs. Follow best practices for authentication, input validation, and protecting sensitive data.

5.Performance Optimization: Optimize the usage of libraries or APIs to enhance performance. Minimize unnecessary requests, cache data when appropriate, and leverage asynchronous programming techniques.

6.Testing and Dependency Management: Write comprehensive tests to validate the behavior of libraries or APIs. Use dependency management tools and techniques to handle library versions and avoid conflicts.

By gaining an overview of popular tools and frameworks, understanding how to choose the right technology stack, and following best practices when working with libraries and APIs, you can optimize your development process, ensure compatibility, and deliver high-quality applications. These practices will enable you to leverage the power of existing resources while maintaining control and customization in your projects.

Chapter VIII. Project-Based Learning

A. Designing and Implementing a Full-Stack Project

Project-based learning is an effective approach to solidify your skills as a full-stack software engineer. By designing and implementing a full-stack project, you can apply your knowledge in a real-world scenario and gain hands-on experience. Here are key steps to guide you through the process:

Project Planning: Define the scope, requirements, and goals of your project. Identify the target audience, functionalities, and technologies you want to incorporate. Break down the project into smaller tasks and create a project timeline.

Backend Development: Begin by setting up the backend infrastructure. Design the database schema and implement data models. Create APIs for data retrieval and modification. Implement business logic and ensure proper error handling. Write unit tests to validate the functionality of backend components.

Frontend Development: Build the frontend interface that will interact with the backend. Design user interfaces using wireframes or UI design tools. Implement responsive layouts, navigation, and user interactions. Integrate with backend APIs to retrieve and manipulate data. Ensure a seamless user experience across different devices and browsers.

Data Flow and Integration: Establish a smooth data flow between the frontend and backend. Test API calls and data synchronization. Handle data validation, transformation, and error scenarios.

Implement mechanisms for real-time updates or notifications, if applicable.

Testing and Quality Assurance: Perform thorough testing to validate the functionality and stability of your application. Write unit tests, integration tests, and end-to-end tests. Conduct usability testing to ensure a smooth user experience. Identify and address any bugs or issues that arise during testing.

B. Step-by-Step Walkthrough of a Practical Application

In this section, we will provide a step-by-step walkthrough of a practical full-stack application. By following this example, you will gain insights into the development process and learn best practices for creating a robust application. Here is an overview of the steps involved:

Project Setup: Set up the development environment, including installing the necessary tools and frameworks. Create the project structure and initialize version control.

Backend Development:

a. Design the database schema and create the necessary tables. b. Implement backend APIs for data retrieval and modification. c. Write backend logic to handle business requirements and ensure proper error handling.

d. Integrate any third-party services or APIs, if required.

Frontend Development:

a. Design the user interface and create wireframes or mockups. b. Implement the frontend using appropriate frameworks and libraries.

c. Integrate with backend APIs to fetch and update data.

d. Implement user interactions, form validation, and error handling on the frontend.

Data Flow and Integration:

a. Test API calls and ensure proper data transmission between frontend and backend.

b. Implement data synchronization mechanisms to handle real-time updates.

c. Handle authentication and authorization to secure sensitive data.

Testing and Deployment:

a. Write comprehensive tests for both backend and frontend components.

b. Conduct usability testing to ensure a smooth user experience.

c. Optimize performance and address any identified issues.

d. Deploy the application to a production environment, ensuring proper configuration and security measures.

C. Applying Best Practices and Industry Standards

Throughout the project development process, it is important to follow best practices and adhere to industry standards. This ensures that your application is scalable, maintainable, and follows established conventions. Here are some best practices to consider:

Code Organization and Modularity: Structure your codebase in a modular and maintainable manner. Separate concerns, use design patterns, and enforce coding standards.

Version Control and Collaboration: Utilize version control systems like Git to track changes, collaborate with team members, and manage code repositories effectively.

Documentation: Document your code, APIs, and project setup for future reference and easier collaboration. Write clear and concise documentation that helps other developers understand and work with your code.

Security and Data Protection: Follow security best practices to protect sensitive data. Implement proper authentication, authorization, and input validation. Securely store and transmit data using encryption techniques.

Performance Optimization: Optimize your application for performance by minimizing load times, optimizing queries, and caching data where appropriate. Follow best practices for frontend and backend performance.

Continuous Integration and Deployment: Automate build processes, testing, and deployment using continuous integration and continuous deployment (CI/CD) pipelines. This ensures a streamlined and efficient development workflow.

By applying best practices and industry standards throughout your project, you will not only create a high-quality application but also develop habits that will benefit your future projects. Project-based learning allows you to combine theory with practical implementation, giving you a comprehensive understanding of the full-stack development process and preparing you for real-world scenarios.

Chapter IX. Continuous Learning and Professional Growth

A. Staying Updated with the Latest Technologies and Trends

Continuous learning is crucial for staying relevant and advancing your skills as a full-stack software engineer. The field of technology is constantly evolving, with new frameworks, tools, and techniques emerging regularly. To ensure your professional growth, it is important to stay updated with the latest technologies and trends. Here are key strategies for staying informed:

Technology News and Blogs: Follow reputable technology news sources, blogs, and websites that provide updates on the latest advancements in backend and frontend development. Examples include TechCrunch, Hacker News, Medium, and industry-specific blogs.

Developer Conferences and Meetups: Attend developer conferences and meetups to learn from industry experts, gain insights into emerging technologies, and network with fellow developers. Keep an eye out for conferences focused on full-stack development, backend and frontend frameworks, and technology trends.

Online Communities and Forums: Join online communities and forums dedicated to software engineering, full-stack development, and specific technologies. Engage in discussions, ask questions, and share your knowledge. Examples include Stack Overflow, Reddit's programming subreddits, and specialized developer forums.

Social Media: Follow influential developers, industry thought leaders, and technology organizations on social media platforms like Twitter, LinkedIn, and GitHub. These platforms often share updates, tutorials, and resources related to backend and frontend development.

Professional Networks: Build and nurture professional networks within the software engineering community. Attend local tech events, join professional associations, and connect with colleagues and mentors. Networking provides opportunities to learn from others, share experiences, and stay informed about industry trends.

B. Participating in Open-Source Projects and Communities

Contributing to open-source projects and communities is an excellent way to enhance your skills, gain practical experience, and collaborate with other developers. By actively participating in open-source projects, you can learn from experienced developers, contribute to meaningful projects, and showcase your abilities. Here are steps to get involved:

Find Relevant Projects: Explore popular open-source projects related to backend or frontend development. Platforms like GitHub provide a vast collection of open-source repositories. Look for projects aligned with your interests and skills.

Start with Small Contributions: Begin by making small contributions, such as fixing bugs, improving documentation, or implementing minor features. This allows you to become familiar with the project's codebase and community guidelines.

Collaborate and Learn: Engage with the project's community and collaborate with other contributors. Ask questions, seek feedback, and learn from the expertise of other developers. Take advantage of code reviews and discussions to improve your coding practices.

Showcase Your Work: Highlight your open-source contributions on your resume, portfolio, or personal website. Potential employers value open-source contributions as they demonstrate your commitment to learning, collaboration, and real-world problem-solving.

C. Leveraging Online Resources for Ongoing Learning

The internet offers a vast array of resources for continuous learning in the field of software engineering. Online platforms provide tutorials, courses, documentation, and interactive exercises that can enhance your knowledge and skills. Here are key resources to leverage:

Online Learning Platforms: Explore platforms like Udemy, Coursera, edX, and Pluralsight, which offer a wide range of online courses covering backend and frontend development. These platforms often provide certifications upon completion, adding credibility to your skillset.

Documentation and Official Guides: Study the documentation and official guides of frameworks, libraries, and programming languages. These resources provide in-depth explanations, usage examples, and best practices directly from the creators of the technology.

YouTube and Video Tutorials: Utilize YouTube and other video-sharing platforms for tutorials and walkthroughs. Many developers and tech influencers create educational content on frontend and backend development, covering various topics and technologies.

Online Coding Challenges and Practice Sites: Engage in coding challenges and practice coding sites like LeetCode, HackerRank, and Codecademy. These platforms offer interactive exercises and real-world scenarios to sharpen your coding skills.

Online Coding Communities: Join online coding communities like GitHub, GitLab, and Bitbucket. Explore open-source projects, collaborate with developers, and learn from shared codebases. Engaging in discussions and code reviews can broaden your knowledge and foster learning.

Remember that continuous learning is a lifelong journey, and it is important to allocate time regularly for self-improvement. Stay curious, explore new technologies, and embrace challenges as opportunities for growth. By staying updated, participating in open-source projects, and leveraging online resources, you can continually enhance your skills and advance your career as a full-stack software engineer.

Chapter X. Career Paths and Opportunities

A. Exploring Various Career Paths for Full-Stack Engineers

As a full-stack software engineer, you have a range of career paths to explore within the field of software development.

Your expertise in both backend and frontend development opens up opportunities across different industries and roles. Here are some career paths to consider:

1.Full-Stack Developer: As a full-stack developer, you can continue to expand your knowledge and skills in both backend and frontend technologies. You'll be responsible for developing end-to-end applications, ensuring smooth integration between the server and client components.

Backend Engineer: Focus primarily on backend development, specializing in server-side technologies, database management, and APIs. Backend engineers build robust, scalable, and secure systems to handle data processing, logic implementation, and server-side operations.

2.Frontend Engineer: Specialize in frontend development, creating visually appealing and user-friendly interfaces. Frontend engineers focus on building responsive web applications, optimizing user experiences, and ensuring cross-browser compatibility.

3.UI/UX Developer: Combine your frontend development skills with user experience (UX) and user interface (UI) design principles. UI/UX developers create interfaces that are not only visually appealing but also intuitive, ensuring seamless user interactions and experiences.

4.Technical Lead/Architect: As your experience grows, you may transition into a leadership role, guiding development teams and making architectural decisions. Technical leads or architects oversee the design and implementation of complex software solutions.

5.Product Manager: Move into a product-focused role, where you work closely with stakeholders to define product vision, gather requirements, and coordinate development efforts. Product managers bridge the gap between business objectives and technical implementation.

B. Job Market Trends and Demand for Versatile Developers

The job market for full-stack engineers is highly promising, with strong demand for professionals who can handle both backend and frontend development. Here are some job market trends and factors that contribute to the demand for versatile developers:

Industry Adaptability: As technology continues to evolve, businesses increasingly seek developers who can adapt and work on different parts of the software stack. Full-stack engineers offer the versatility needed to address changing business needs.

Agile Development Practices: Agile methodologies have become the industry standard for software development, emphasizing cross-functional teams and flexibility. Full-stack engineers are well-suited to agile environments, contributing to all aspects of a project's lifecycle.

Startups and Small Companies: Startups and small companies often have limited resources and require developers who can handle multiple responsibilities. Full-stack engineers are valuable in such settings, as they can take ownership of the entire development process.

Freelancing and Consulting Opportunities: Full-stack engineers have the flexibility to work as freelancers or consultants, offering their expertise to multiple clients or projects. This allows for diverse work experiences and the ability to specialize in specific domains.

Remote Work Opportunities: The rise of remote work and distributed teams has created more opportunities for full-stack engineers. The ability to handle both backend and frontend development allows for effective collaboration in remote settings.

C. Advancement Opportunities and Potential Future Roles

As a full-stack software engineer, there are numerous advancement opportunities and potential future roles to pursue. Here are some possibilities for career growth:

Senior Engineer/Technical Lead: With experience and expertise, you can advance to senior engineer or technical lead roles. These positions involve leading development teams, mentoring junior engineers, and making technical decisions.

Engineering Manager: Transition into a management role, where you oversee a team of developers, coordinate projects, and provide strategic guidance.

Engineering managers balance technical expertise with people management skills.

Solution Architect: Specialize in designing complex software solutions, considering architectural patterns, scalability, security, and performance. Solution architects work closely with stakeholders to ensure effective technical implementations.

DevOps Engineer: Extend your skill set into DevOps practices, focusing on automation, deployment, and infrastructure management. DevOps engineers bridge the gap between development and operations, ensuring efficient and reliable software delivery.

Entrepreneurship: As a full-stack engineer, you have the potential to start your own tech company or work on innovative projects. Your versatile skill set allows you to drive the entire development process and bring your ideas to life.

Specialization: While full-stack development provides a broad skill set, you may choose to specialize in a specific area over time. This could involve becoming an expert in a particular backend framework, frontend library, or emerging technology.

As you progress in your career, it's important to continue learning, staying updated with industry trends, and adapting to evolving technologies. This will enable you to seize new opportunities and expand your skill set, positioning yourself for a fulfilling and successful career as a full-stack software engineer.

Chapter XI. Conclusion

A. Recap of Key Concepts Covered in the Book

Throughout this book, we have explored the path to becoming a proficient full-stack software engineer, capable of handling both backend and frontend development. Let's recap the key concepts covered:

Understanding the Demand: We delved into the growing demand for versatile software engineers who can bridge the gap between backend and frontend development. We explored the advantages of being a full-stack engineer and the value it brings to businesses.

Building a Strong Foundation: We emphasized the importance of building a strong foundation in programming concepts, essential web development technologies, and data structures and algorithms. These fundamentals serve as the building blocks of your technical knowledge.

Backend Development: We explored backend technologies and frameworks, database management and design principles, server-side scripting, and security considerations. These topics equipped you with the skills to develop robust and secure backend systems.

Frontend Development: We discussed frontend technologies and frameworks, UI design principles, responsive and accessible web interfaces, and integrating backend functionality with the frontend. These topics empowered you to create engaging and user-friendly frontend experiences.

Bridging the Gap: Full-Stack Development: We examined the interplay between backend and frontend, creating seamless integration between the two layers, and managing data flow and communication. These insights enabled you to develop end-to-end applications with cohesive user experiences.

Tools, Frameworks, and Libraries: We explored popular tools and frameworks for both backend and frontend development, discussed how to choose the right technology stack, and provided best practices for working with common libraries and APIs. These insights empowered you to leverage the right tools and resources effectively.

Project-Based Learning: We emphasized the importance of project-based learning, providing guidance on designing and implementing a full-stack project, offering a step-by-step walkthrough, and encouraging the application of best practices and industry standards. These lessons reinforced your practical skills and problem-solving abilities.

Continuous Learning and Professional Growth: We discussed the significance of continuous learning, participation in open-source projects and communities, and leveraging online resources for ongoing learning. These strategies ensure that you remain up-to-date and continually enhance your skills as a full-stack engineer.

Career Paths and Opportunities: We explored various career paths for full-stack engineers, analyzed job market trends, and highlighted advancement opportunities and potential future roles. These insights opened up a world of possibilities for your professional growth.

B. Encouragement and Guidance for Aspiring Full-Stack Engineers

To aspiring full-stack engineers, I commend your dedication and passion for the field of software development. Becoming a proficient full-stack engineer is a journey that requires perseverance and continuous learning. Embrace challenges, seek opportunities to expand your skills, and stay curious about emerging technologies.

Remember that success in this field is not solely measured by technical expertise. Effective communication, collaboration, and problem-solving skills are equally important. Cultivate these soft skills to complement your technical prowess and become a well-rounded professional.

Seek out mentorship and guidance from experienced developers who can provide insights and help navigate your career path. Actively participate in the developer community, attend conferences, and engage in discussions.

These connections will broaden your perspective, foster growth, and open doors to new opportunities.

C. Final Thoughts and Next Steps for Readers

As you reach the conclusion of this book, I encourage you to reflect on your journey and the knowledge you have acquired. Take pride in your accomplishments thus far and embrace the excitement of what lies ahead. The world of full-stack development is dynamic and ever-evolving, offering endless possibilities for innovation and growth.

Continue your learning journey by staying updated with industry trends, exploring new technologies, and honing your existing skills. Seek out real-world projects and challenges that allow you to apply your knowledge and expand your portfolio. Embrace a growth mindset and view setbacks as opportunities for learning and improvement.

Remember, becoming a proficient full-stack software engineer is a lifelong pursuit. Embrace continuous learning and adapt to the changing landscape of technology. Embrace the joy of creating impactful software solutions, collaborating with teams, and making a positive impact in the world through your work.

Congratulations on completing this book! I wish you the utmost success in your journey to becoming a skilled and sought-after full-stack software engineer. May your passion for learning, dedication to excellence, and commitment to growth propel you towards a fulfilling and successful career in the exciting field of full-stack development.